# Purim

By Adam D. Fisher
Illustrated by Jana Paiss

Behrman House

Purim feels like jumping around
and making lots of noise.

Purim feels like
cookies
called hamantashen.
How many
will you eat?

Purim feels like
wearing a costume.
No one will know
who you are!

Purim feels like
hearing a story of a king and a queen
and a very mean man.

Long ago and far away
there lived a queen.
Her name was Esther.
She was very beautiful
and very brave.
Esther lived in a castle
with golden halls
and silver walls.

In the garden there were
flowers and birds.
There were soft cats and furry dogs
and a big white horse.

One day, Esther's cousin Mordecai
came to tell her
that a very mean man named Haman
wanted to hurt Esther and all the Jews.
Haman wanted to hurt our people.

Queen Esther spoke
to the king and told him
what Haman wanted to do.
The king was angry
at Haman, and stopped
him from hurting the Jews.

וַיְהִי בִּימֵי אֲחַשְׁוֵרוֹשׁ הוּא אֲחַשְׁוֵרוֹשׁ הַמֹּלֵךְ מֵהֹדּוּ וְעַד־כּוּשׁ שֶׁבַע וְעֶשְׂרִים וּמֵאָה מְדִינָה. בַּיָּמִים הָהֵם כְּשֶׁבֶת הַמֶּלֶךְ אֲחַשְׁוֵרוֹשׁ עַל כִּסֵּא מַלְכוּתוֹ אֲשֶׁר בְּשׁוּשַׁן הַבִּירָה. בִּשְׁנַת שָׁלוֹשׁ לְמָלְכוּ עָשָׂה מִשְׁתֶּה

Our people were very happy.
So every Purim we tell this story.
We read the story from a special
book called the Megillah.

When you hear the name Haman,
make lots of noise with your gragger,
to boo the man who tried to hurt us.

You can yell
and shout and
stamp your feet,
bang pots and
pans and big
empty cans.

You can wear a funny costume.
Which will you get ready—
a king, a queen,
a dancer or a teddy?

You can eat hamantashen.

Purim cookies have three sides.
They are filled with good things
like raspberries, poppy seeds
and prune jam.

When we are happy
we want other people
to feel happy too.

So we send
Purim treats,
called *shalaḥ manot,*
to our friends;
we give money
to help the poor.